MACHINES ★ AT WORK

DIGGERS

BY MARV ALINAS

THE CHILD'S WORLD® • MANKATO, MINNESOTA

The
Child's
World®

Published in the United States of America by The Child's World®
1980 Lookout Drive • Mankato, MN 56003-1705
800-599-READ • www.childsworld.com

PHOTO CREDITS

© Construction Photography/Corbis: 16
© David M. Budd Photography: 12
© Gunter Marx/Alamy: 19
© iStockphoto.com/Bjorn Heller: 3
© iStockphoto.com/Bonnie Schupp: 7
© iStockphoto.com/Brian Nolan: 8
© iStockphoto.com/Guillermo Perales Gonzalez: 4
© iStockphoto.com/Paul Vasarhelyi: 15
© iStockphoto.com/Trevor Fisher: 11
© iStockphoto.com/Vasiliki Varvaki: cover, 2, 20

ACKNOWLEDGMENTS

The Child's World®: Mary Berendes, Publishing Director;
Katherine Stevenson, Editor

The Design Lab: Design and Page Production

LIBRARY OF CONGRESS CATALOGING-IN-PUBLICATION DATA

Alinas, Marv.
  Diggers / by Marv Alinas.
    p. cm. — (Machines at work)
  Includes bibliographical references and index.
  ISBN 978-1-59296-948-7 (library bound: alk. paper)
  1. Excavating machinery–Juvenile literature. I. Title. II. Series.
  TA735.A4464 2007
  624.1'52–dc22   2007013399

Contents

You can see this digger's powerful scoop.

What are diggers?

Diggers are power shovels or **excavators**. These powerful machines dig and scoop. They dig holes in the ground. They scoop up dirt and rock. They drop the dirt in piles. They place the dirt in trucks or train cars.

What are diggers used for?

Diggers are used for many jobs. Some dig holes where buildings will go. Some dig **trenches** for pipes or wires. Some scoop up rock in **mines**. Others dig out dirt and sand to make rivers deeper.

This digger is smaller. It is digging a trench for pipes.

Hurricane Katrina destroyed this house. A digger is cleaning up the mess left behind.

Diggers help clean up areas, too. Sometimes people tear down old buildings. Sometimes storms destroy buildings. Diggers help tear the buildings down. They help clean up the mess. They load the heavy trash on trucks. The trash goes to the dump.

What are the parts of a digger?

Diggers have a long arm called a **boom**. The end of the arm holds a big metal **bucket**. Together, the bucket and boom are called a **backhoe**. The digger pulls the boom in. That makes the bucket scoop up dirt.

backhoe

boom

bucket

You can see this digger's huge backhoe parts.

A digger's cab has a seat for the driver. Windows let the driver see in every direction.

The digger's body has a **cab** where the driver sits. The cab can spin all the way around. The cab has lots of **controls**. Some controls make the digger go forward and backward. Other controls move the boom and bucket.

Some diggers move around on wheels. But most diggers move on metal or rubber belts. These belts are called **crawler tracks**. Crawler tracks help diggers move over bumpy ground. They keep diggers from sinking in sand or mud.

Heavy crawler tracks help keep this digger from tipping over.

This machine digs up dirt from river bottoms. Its boom is extra long to reach deeper areas.

Are there different kinds of diggers?

Diggers come in many shapes and sizes. Mini excavators are small diggers for small jobs. Bigger excavators are used for bigger jobs. You often see these diggers where people are building things.

Some excavators are very large. Dragline excavators often work in mines. They take huge bites of rock and dirt. The biggest diggers of all are bucket-wheel excavators. They are some of the biggest machines in the world!

This huge bucket-wheel excavator is used in a Canadian mine.

This digger is moving dirt to make way for a new building.

Are diggers important?

Diggers are very important. They are used all over the world. They do all kinds of hard jobs. Nothing digs and scoops as well as a digger!

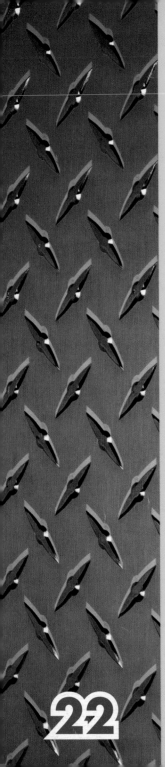

Glossary

backhoe (BAK-hoh) A backhoe is a digging scoop on a long arm.

boom (BOOM) A boom is a long arm that holds something up.

bucket (BUH-ket) A digger's bucket is a big metal scoop.

cab (KAB) A machine's cab is the area where the driver sits.

controls (kun-TROHLZ) Controls are parts that people use to run a machine.

crawler tracks (KRAW-lur TRAX) Crawler tracks are metal belts that some machines use for moving.

excavators (EX-kuh-vay-turz) Excavators are digging machines with a body that spins around.

mines (MYNZ) Mines are places where people dig rock from underground.

trenches (TREN-chez) Trenches are long, narrow ditches.

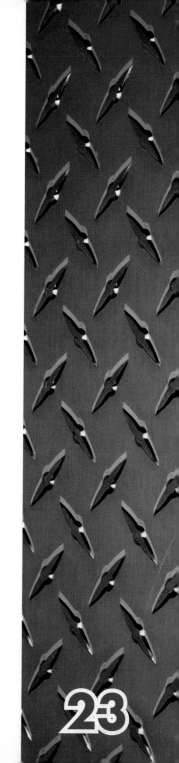

Books

Deschamps, Nicola. *Digger*. New York: DK Publishing, 2006.

Royston, Angela, and Philippe Dupasquier. *The Story of a Digger*. London: Kingfisher, 1998.

Young, Caroline. *Diggers*. London: Usborne Publishing, 1992.

Young, Caroline, Steve Page, Teri Gower (illustrator), Nick Hawker (illustrator), and Chris Lyon (illustrator). *Diggers and Cranes*. London: Usborne Publishing, 2005.

Web Sites

Visit our Web page for lots of links about diggers:
http://www.childsworld.com/links
Note to parents, teachers, and librarians: We routinely check our Web links to make sure they're safe, active sites—so encourage your readers to check them out!

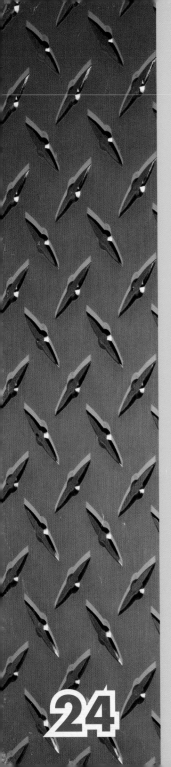

 # Index

 # About the Author

Marv Alinas has lived in Minnesota for over thirty years. When she's not reading or writing, Marv enjoys spending time with her dog and traveling to small river towns in northeastern Iowa and western Wisconsin.